The
Do-It-Yourself
Lettering Book

Anna Burgess

Illustrated by Kim Gamble

WATERMILL PRESS

The Do-It-Yourself Lettering Book
First published in the United States in 1993
by Watermill Press

Copyright © Anna Burgess and
Lineup Pty Limited 1991

Cataloguing-in-Publication data:

  Burgess, Anna.
    The do-it-yourself lettering book.

    ISBN 0 646 03995 4.

    1. Calligraphy – Juvenile literature.
    2. Lettering – Juvenile literature.
    I. Gamble, Kim.
    II. Title

745.6

Assembly by Just James Studio
Typeset by The Type Workshop
Cover design by Kim Gamble

10 9 8 7 6 5 4 3 2

YOU are special, individual, unique . . .
The way you speak is special, individual,
unique . . .
This book shows how to make what you
WRITE special, individual, unique.
It's called the **DO-IT-YOURSELF
LETTERING BOOK**
because you **CAN** do it yourself!
Whether you are preparing a project
for school, making a poster, or
creating a card for a friend, you can
turn something ordinary into
something super special using
the ideas in this book.

The DO-IT-YOURSELF
LETTERING BOOK
will help you.
And here's how . . .

DOOR SIGNS

ENTINES

LETTERS

OKMARKS

AWARDS

PROJECTS   BOOK COVERS   BIRTHDAY CARDS   SCROLLS

D.I.Y. POSTERS   D.I.Y. CALENDARS   D.I.Y. DIARIES   LABELS   CERTIFICATES

DECORATED POEMS

MOTHER'S DAY CARDS

TITLE PAGES   CHAPTER HEADINGS   CHRISTMAS CARDS   GET WELL CARDS   GIFT CARDS

FATHER'S DAY CARDS   EASTER CARDS   INSTRUCTIONS

CONTENTS

CREATIVE LETTERING

**P**eople have been doing creative lettering for thousands of years. Beginning letters like the one at the start of this paragraph were called illuminated letters and were often decorated with real gold.
(Now that's creative lettering!)

You can see some modern examples in the section "Beautiful Beginnings."

All of the Ten Commandments have been made to fit on a one cent coin.
(Now that's creative lettering!)
Thousands of years ago, the Egyptians wrote with pictographs and people are still reading them.

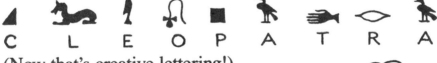

C   L   E   O   P   A   T   R   A

(Now that's creative lettering!)

Famous artists such as Andy Warhol used creative lettering in their paintings – and an Andy Warhol painting sells for hundreds of thousands of dollars.
(Now is that creative lettering . . . or what?)

BUT...

you don't have to be a genius or a great artist to use DO-IT-YOURSELF LETTERING. In your toolbox you will need . . .

Blank sheets or books (graph paper is great)

Pens

Erasers (and maybe white correction fluid.)

A ruler (a parallel ruler can be very helpful)

Coloring materials (crayons, inks, colored pencils, poster paints, water colors, felt-nibbed pens)

REMEMBER that with DO-IT-YOURSELF LETTERING there's no RIGHT way. Your way is the RIGHT way as long as it communicates your message.

The two most common formats are portrait (above) and landscape (below).
Choose the one that will best enhance your project.

Other points to consider: borders;
a strong, clear picture which can be a cut out from a
magazine, a hand-colored photocopy or your own drawing;
a strong, clear heading.

Combine the elements in a few different ways before deciding which design to use.

PAGE LAYOUTS

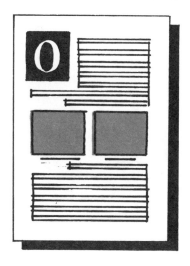

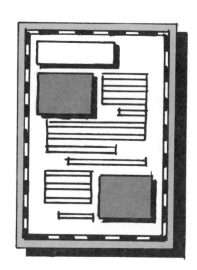

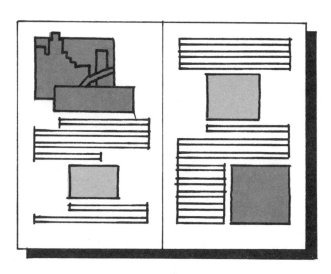

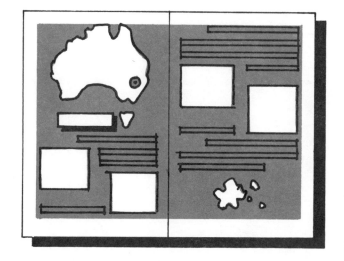

Points to consider: borders;
the balance of pictures and writing
across the page or double spread;
captions;
cutouts;
panels for headings and
sub-headings;
the use of color.

Points to consider: cutouts;
the size of the
card (especially
if you want to mail it).

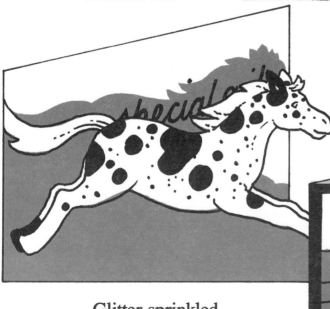

Glitter sprinkled
on a thin layer of
glue can be
effective too.

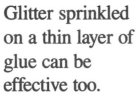

9

PUTTING IT ALL TOGETHER

- These pages show how the ideas in this book might be used for a project – in this case, a wall poster on Endangered Species.
- First, gather all your material together.

SUBJECT NOTES

Pictures

Cardboard, pens, scissors etc.

GLUE

Sketch several different ideas on a spare sheet.

Idea #1:
Landscape format.

Decorated letter.

Colored border.

ENDANGERED SPECIES

Symmetrical layout – neat but perhaps a bit boring.

Border isn't quite right for the subject.

Idea #2: Portrait format.
The heading has been moved; the decorated letter stays; the text is broken up into shorter, more readable blocks. Some of the pictures have been cut out and pasted over the border for a more dramatic effect.

A simple zig-zag pattern is all the border needs.

ENDANGERED SPECIES

SUMMARY

Layout is moved around to create a more interesting design.

Too much text in the middle – maybe a diagram would be better.

A panel makes the summary stand out.

10

GRIDDING

This signwriter worked out how to fit the letters on this huge billboard by using gridding.

Beautiful Skies AIRPORT

This **DO-IT-YOURSELF** signwriter is transferring or copying a special letter shape onto a piece of paper, using grids.

In fact, when it comes to DO-IT-YOURSELF LETTERING, graph paper is great. You can make your own by ruling equally-spaced lines vertically (up) and horizontally (across) on a blank sheet of paper – or you can use the grids on the inside cover of this book.

You can also use tracing paper to copy the images in this book.

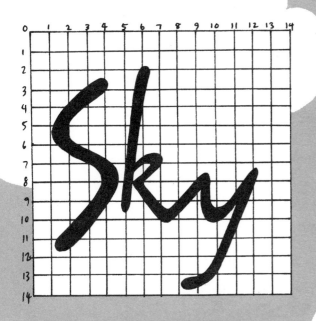

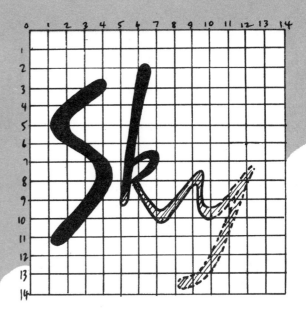

SAMPLE GRID

Count the squares in the sample on which the letter falls. Count across and down. On your own gridded paper, copy, square by square, the shape and placement of the letter.

You can work from BIG grid

to small

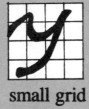

small grid

to big

or, as the sample shows, same size to same size, just as long as you count correctly.

BASIC LETTERING STYLES

The English alphabet has 26 letters and each letter has two forms, so there are: 26 CAPITAL
(or UPPERCASE) letters and
26 small
(or lowercase) letters.

Each letter has a basic shape.

Letters can be freestanding – PRINTED

or joined – *Cursive*

Letters can be further divided into two main groups: serif and sans serif (sans serif means 'without' a serif). The serif is the little stroke you see at the end of each line in letters such as E. Notice that the thickness of the lines in serif lettering alternates from thick to thin, whereas in sans serif lettering the thickness of each stroke is generally uniform.

SERIF

E

LETTER WITH SERIF

E

LETTER WITHOUT SERIF

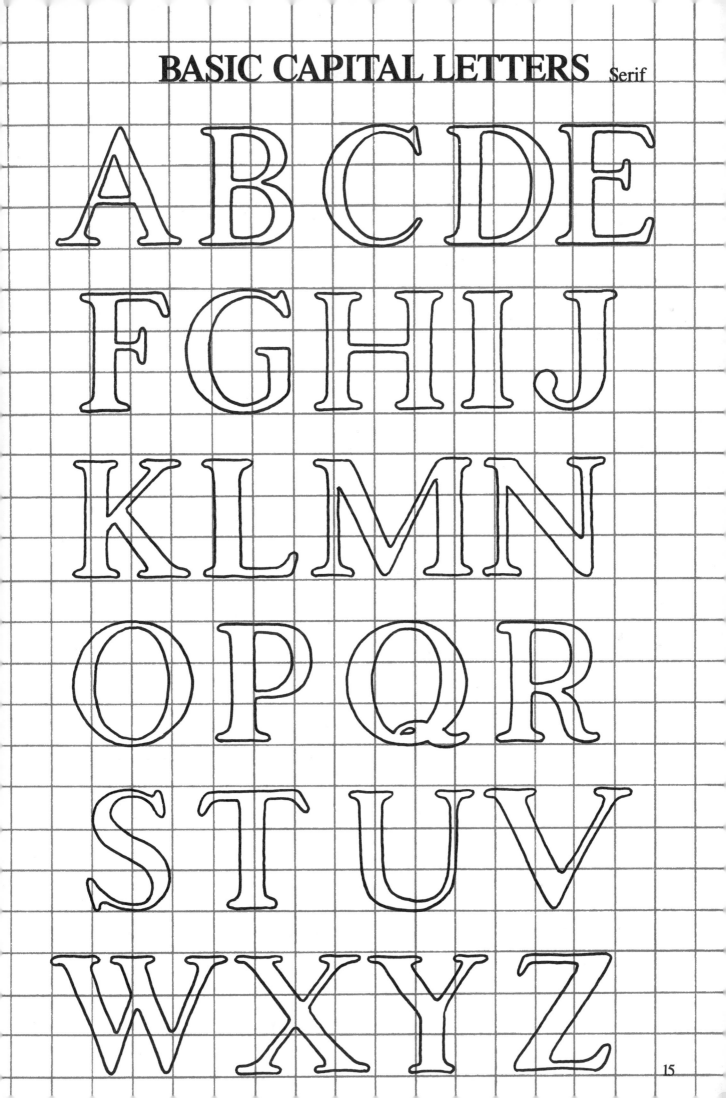

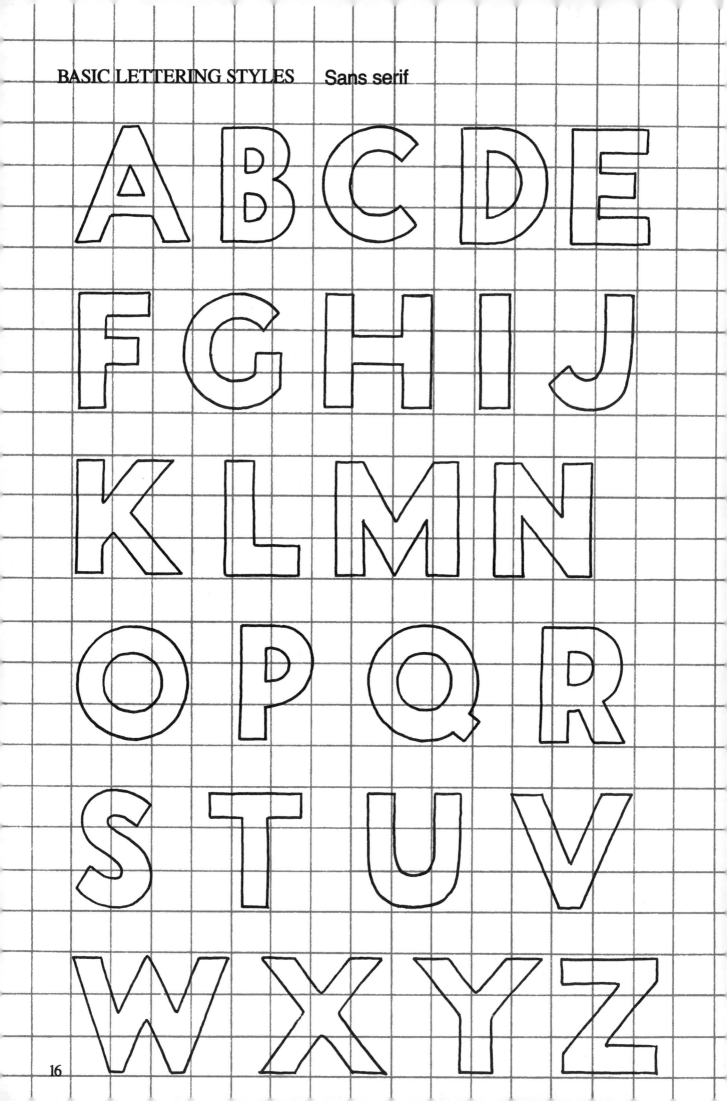

A Three-dimensional **A** Three-dimensional reversed **A** Repeated **A** Shadowed

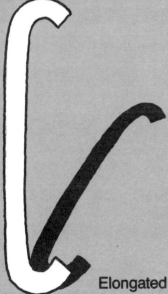

Laid back **B** Reflected

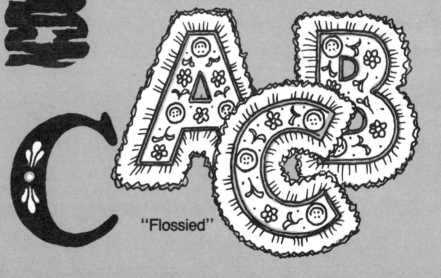

Squashed

Elongated

"Flossied"

D

Broken

D

Patterned

17

Sans serif

abcdefghi
jklmnopq
rstuvwxyz

Serif

abcdefghi
jklmnopq
rstuvwxyz

TREATMENTS – lower case

Three-dimensional reversed

Shadowed

Three-dimensional

Laid back

Repeated

Broken

Patterned

19

lettering can be

thin or TALL

FAT or THICK

WIDE

OVERLAPPING

S · E · P · A · R · A · T · E · D

Sloping Sloping

PATTERNED

WRINKLED

Spotted

STRIPED

checked

WOBBLY

WHITE

BLACK

or coloured

BE VERY

Aa
adorable
Africa
AQUARIUS
Ants

Bb
BLAST
BALLONS
BRICKS
BIRTHDAY
BOG

CONSERVATION
Cc
CHINA
cat
CHANGE
cheers!

Dd
d.t
Darling
DANGER!
DOWN

Ee
echo)))))
EASTER
ELEPHANT
easy

Ff
FIRE
Feel
freedom
FEET

Gg
GREAT
Green
Go!
gold

Hh
Happy
hi
Haunted House
HELP!

24

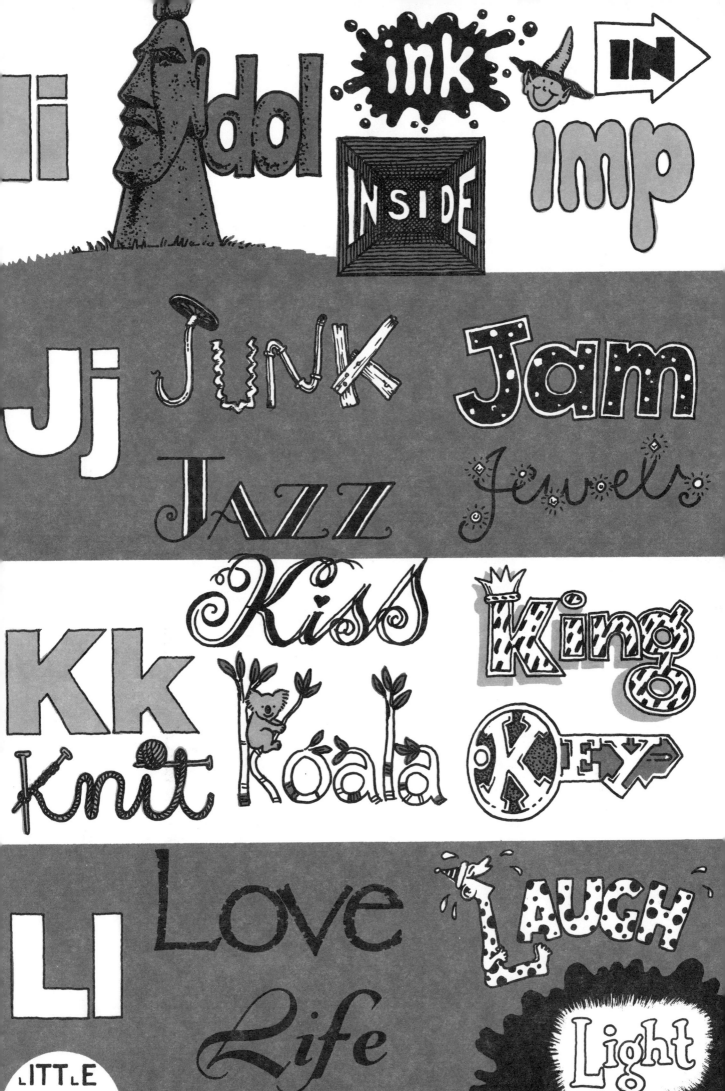

Ii

Idol

ink

IN

imp

INSIDE

Jj

JUNK

Jam

JAZZ

Jewel

Kk

Kiss

King

Knit

Koala

KEY

Ll

Love

LAUGH

Life

Light

LITTLE

Mm

Milk

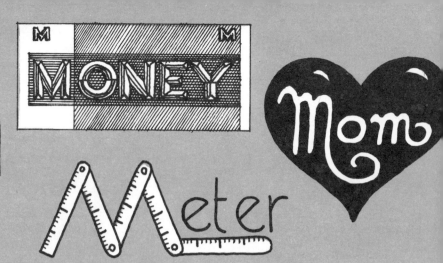

MONEY

Mom

Meter

Nn

NEW

Nasty

night

NoNseNsE

NO

Oo

Orange

ONE

Ornate

VER

OWL

Pp

Pirates!

Prize

PAPER

PULL

PEACE

Quiet

Qq

Quiz

Question

QUIT

Reading

Rr

RR ICH

RIP!

rot

RUINS

SUPER

Ss

Summertime

SUBMARINE

Sorry...

Tea

TASMAN

Tt

TOYS

Two

terrific

Uu

UNDER

UNDONE

UP

UNITE

useful

Vv

VIBRATE

VEGETABLES

Pain

vine

Ww

WINDOW

WAR

WOW!

Xx

X-RAY

XMAS

Yy

Yes!

YETI

YO-YO

Zz

ZIP

ZZZZ

ZODIAC

ZEBRA

ALPHABETS

LETTERING THEMES AND WORD PICTURES

Each of the letters in the English alphabet has a basic shape. No matter how creative you get, you need to be able to identify that basic shape so that your writing has meaning. You can create a whole new alphabet to fit any theme you like.

Thematic alphabets can be used in many ways, such as headings for poems and stories or special signs and messages. On the opposite page, you'll find a DO-IT-YOURSELF alphabet that you could use to decorate an "Autumn" poem or project.

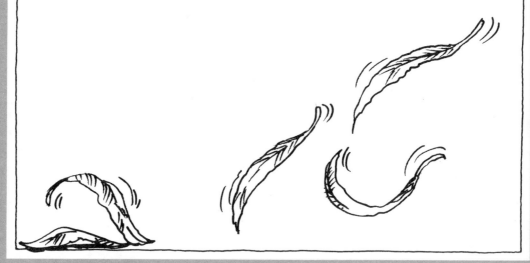

A B C D E
F G H I J
K L M N
O P Q R
S T U V
W X Y Z

A B C D E
F G H I J K
L M N O
P Q R S
T U V W
X Y Z

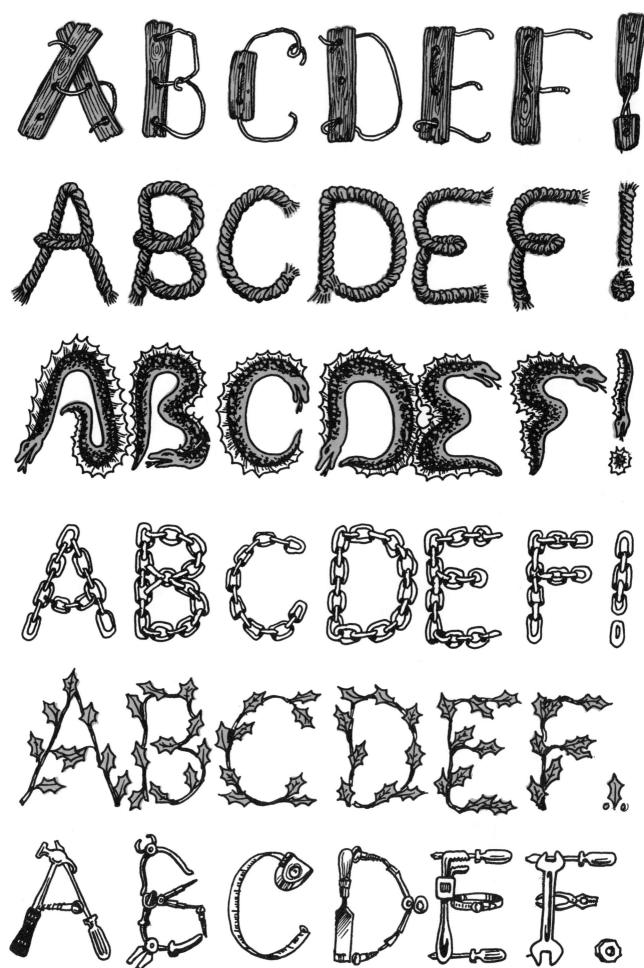

Have fun with
WORD PICTURES

Letters can be made to suggest meaning . . .

Letters can be fitted into shapes to suggest meaning . . .

Words included in the WORD PICTURE pages that follow will give you ideas for making other words.

MOLTEN LAVA

ice cream

oil slime

MELTING

DRIP

VOLCANO LAVA

ASH

ERUPTION CRACK

RUMBLE

ROAR

ROCK STRATA

EARTHQUAKE

Tennis

DIVING

SWIMMING

JOGGING

fishing

SKIPPING

AEROBICS

ATHLETICS

Soccer

basketball

HOCKEY

EQUESTRIAN

39

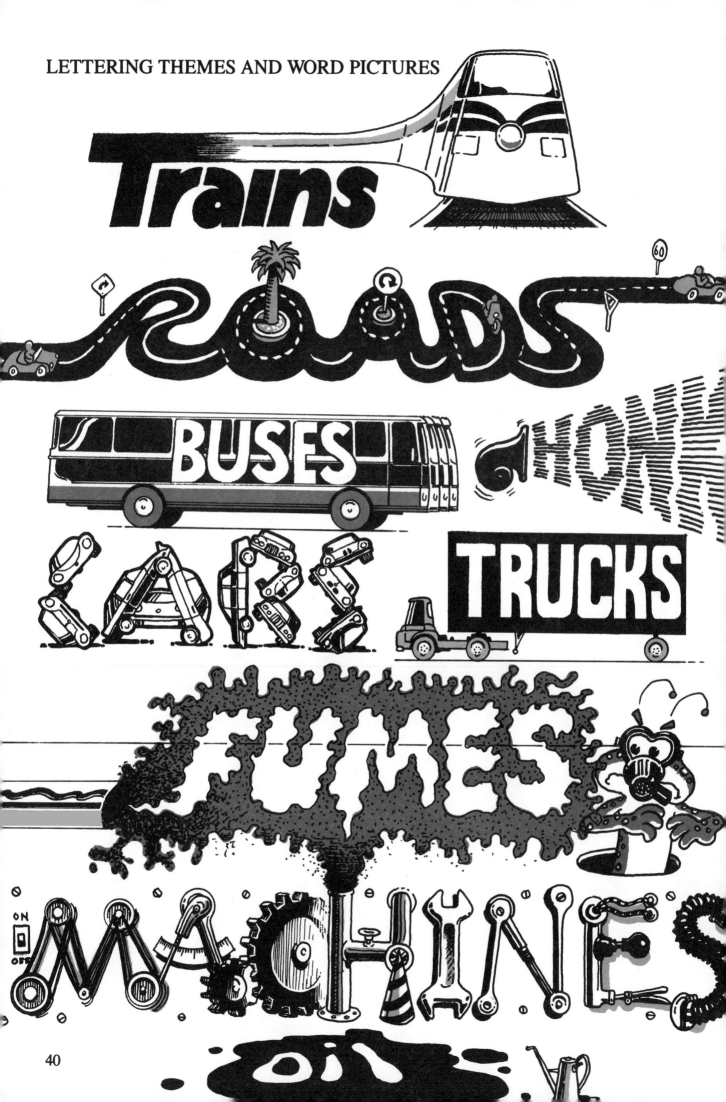

Trains

roads

BUSES

HONK

CARS

TRUCKS

FUMES

MACHINES

OIL

RAIN

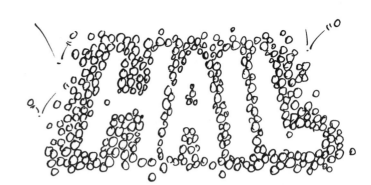

THUNDER

LIGHTNING

WATER

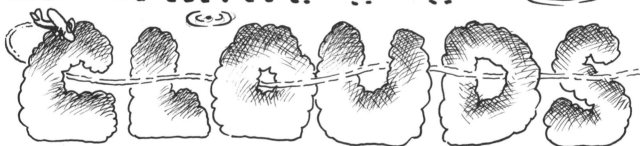
CLOUDS

MIST

WIND

SNOW

MUD

AUSTRALIA

NEW ZEALAND

ENGLAND

JAPAN

ITALY

HOLLAND

U.S.A.

FIJI

FRANCE

SEWING

Pins

Silk

Darning

Lace

wool

Scissors

Button

Embroidery

SHORELINE

yacht

FISH

Sand

SHELLS

SANDCASTLE

bucket

starfish

SHARK!

waves

island

WINDSURFER

ALTERNATE

BALL

BAL ANCE

CATERPILLAR

WIPER

FLY

HEAVY

Light

JUMP

FIELD

SMILE

FROWN

Tree

COPY
COPY

SPOOK

46

SPRING

RELAX

agog

DDD
DDD
DDD

BUILD

HOLE

MULTIPLY

Illusions

TIMBERLANDS

eye ♥ u

SLIDE

Happy Birthday

Happy Birthday

Many Happy Returns

Have a Great Day!

HAPPY MOTHER'S DAY

Happy New Year

CONGRATULATIONS

Congratulations

Season's Greetings

MERRY CHRISTMAS

JOY

Wish you were Here

be my Valentine

BON VOYAGE!

good luck

TAKE CARE

HAVE A HAPPY DAY

Beautiful
Beginnings...

A B C D E F
G H I J K L
M N O P Q
R S T U V
W X Y Z

abcdefghijklmn
opqrstuvwxyz

Once upon a time...

A

The owl and the pussycat

Clouded with snow...

WHAT IS THIS LIFE IF, FULL OF CARE...

Far off a lonely hound

NUMERALS

1234567890

1234567890

1234567890

1234567890

1234567890

1234567890

1234567890

1234567890

1234567890

1234567890

1234567890
1234567890
1234567890
1234567890
1234567890
1234567890
1234567890
123456789
1234567890
1234567890

BORDERS

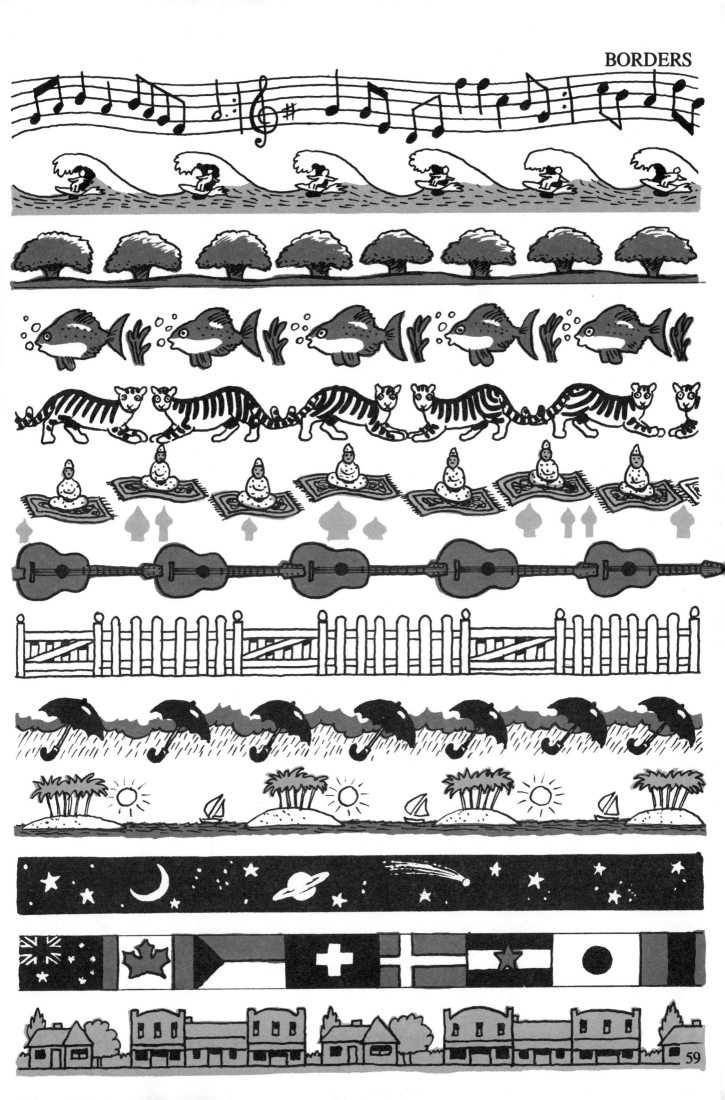

1. PENCIL   2. PENCIL   3. PENCIL   4. PEN   5. ERASE PENCIL

REWARDS

A+

GOOD

✔

Yes!

1st

1

FIRST
CLASS

✔

Thankyou

Well
Done!

Good Work

Finis

CONCLUSION

THE END